ANIMALS BORN ALIVE AND WELL

BY RUTH HELLER

Winter, Spring, Summer, Fall…

Snowshoe Hare

a HARE'S hair changes with them all.

With
love
to
PAUL
and
PHILIP

ANIMALS BORN ALIVE AND WELL

BY RUTH HELLER

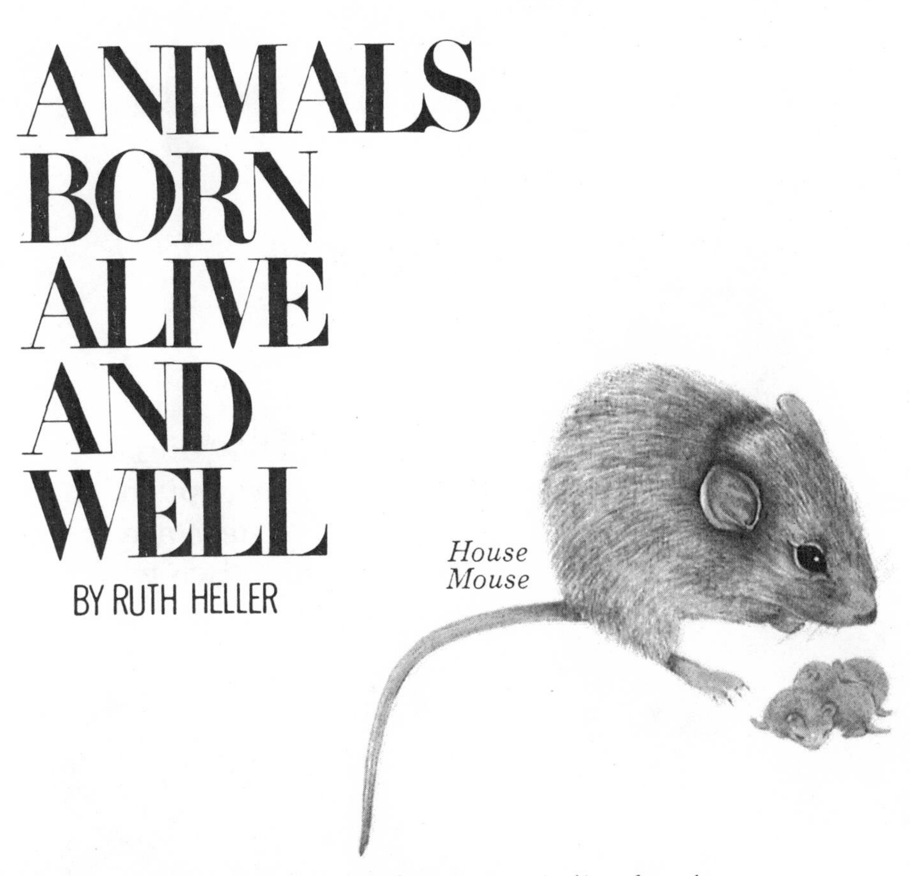

ISBN 0-590-41253-1.

12 11 10 9 8 7 6 5 4 0 1 2/9

Printed in the U.S.A. 23

First Scholastic printing, October 1987

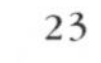

SCHOLASTIC INC.
New York Toronto London Auckland Sydney

MAMMALS
are
animals with fur or hair
who nurse their young
and breathe fresh air.

They don't lay eggs
except these two.
These are the only
two who do.

Spiny Anteater

They
don't
lay
eggs,
as
I have
said,
they're
born
alive and well
instead.

Duckbill Platypus

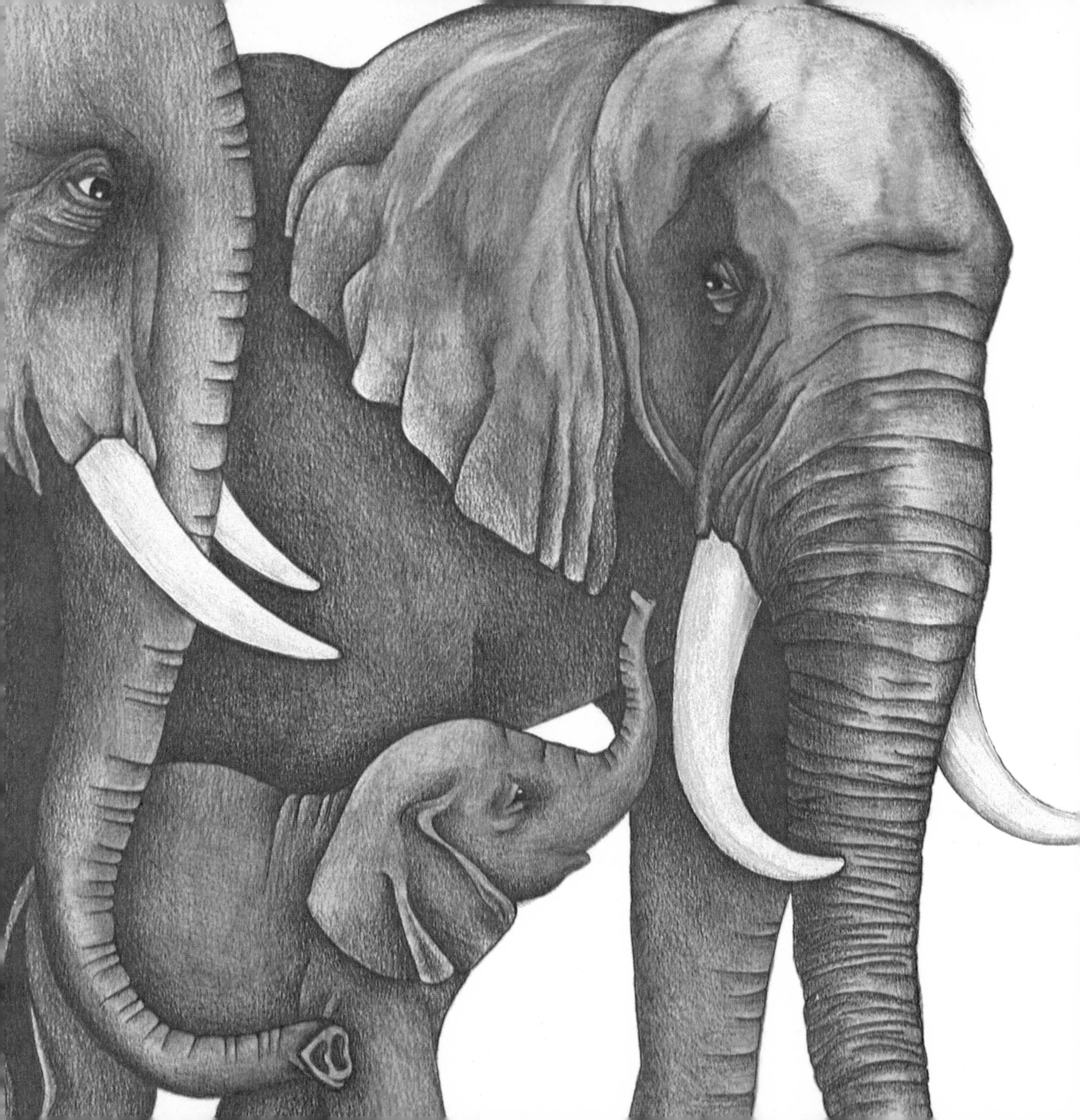

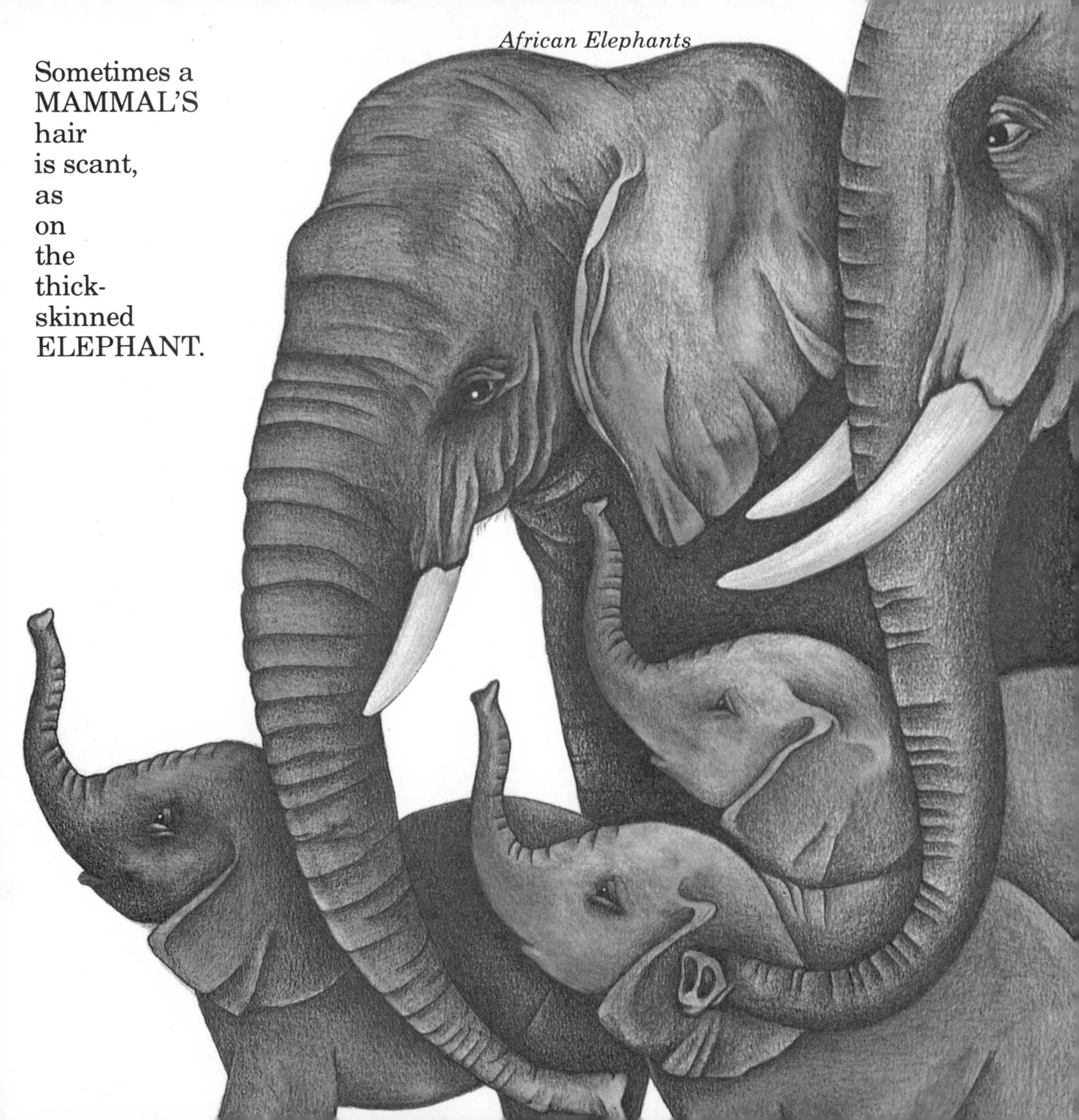

African Elephants

Sometimes a
MAMMAL'S
hair
is scant,
as
on
the
thick-
skinned
ELEPHANT.

Pekinese

Yorkshire Terrier

But here's a pair with hair,

Okapi
Zebra
Ring-tailed
Lemur

and
here
are
lots
with
stripes
and
spots.

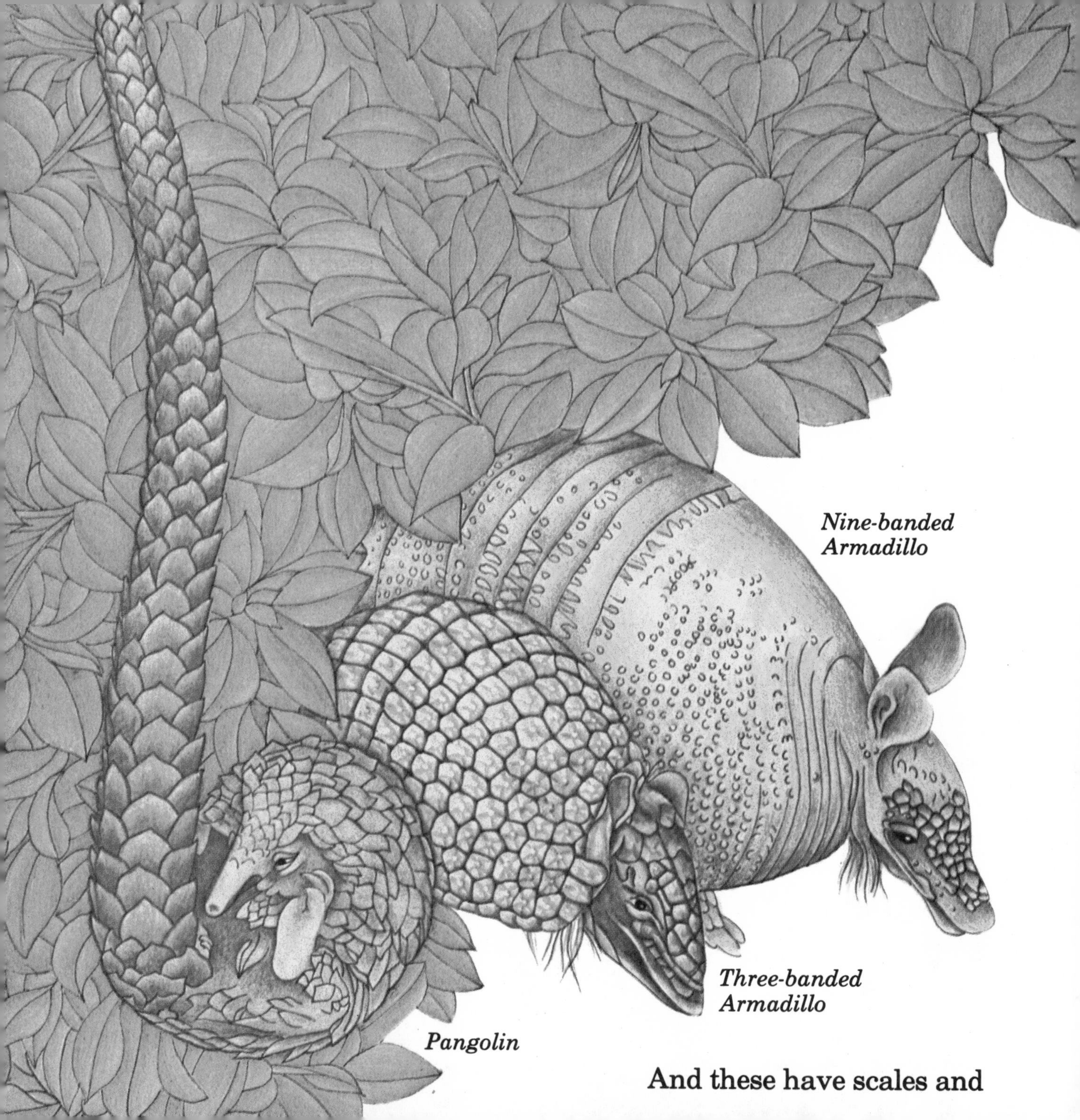

And these have scales and

Porcupine

spikes like nails... but all of them are MAMMALS.

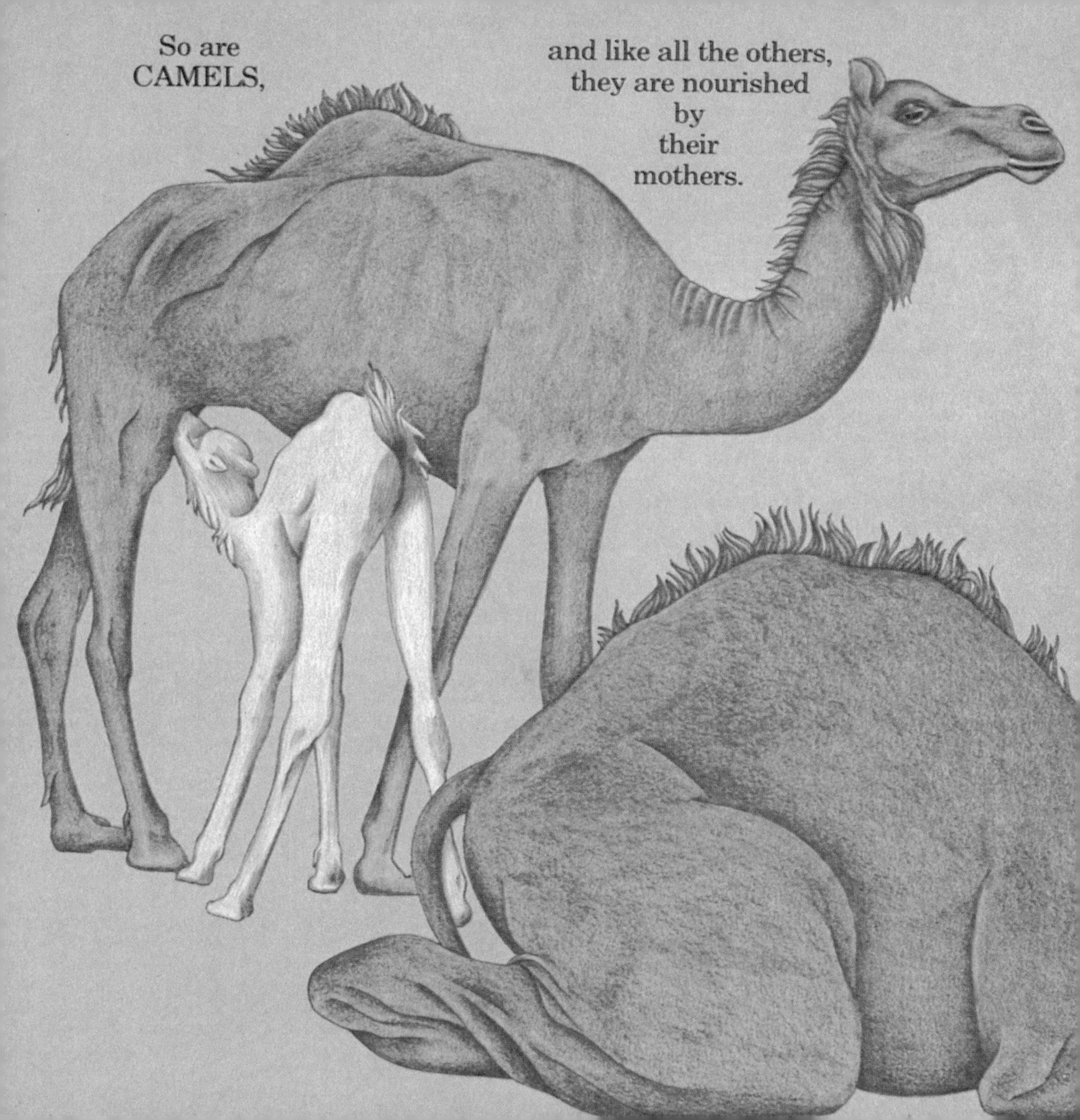

So are
CAMELS,

and like all the others,
they are nourished
by
their
mothers.

Dromedaries

Gazelle

MAMMALS
wild
and...
Deer
Stoat

MAMMALS
tame

all do more or less the same.

When they are
very, very small
into their
mother's pouch
they crawl
and grow
just like this
KANGAROO.

MARSUPIALS
are different
but they are
MAMMALS,
too.

KOALAS
are
MARSUPIALS, too.

MAMMALS
all
breathe air,
you
understand.

This
isn't
hard
for
those
on
land,
or
even
those
found...

Fallow Deer
Wild Goat
Bison
Red Fox
Hippopotamus
Giant Anteater
Prairie Dog

underground…

or those who fly,

Bat

or climb up high.

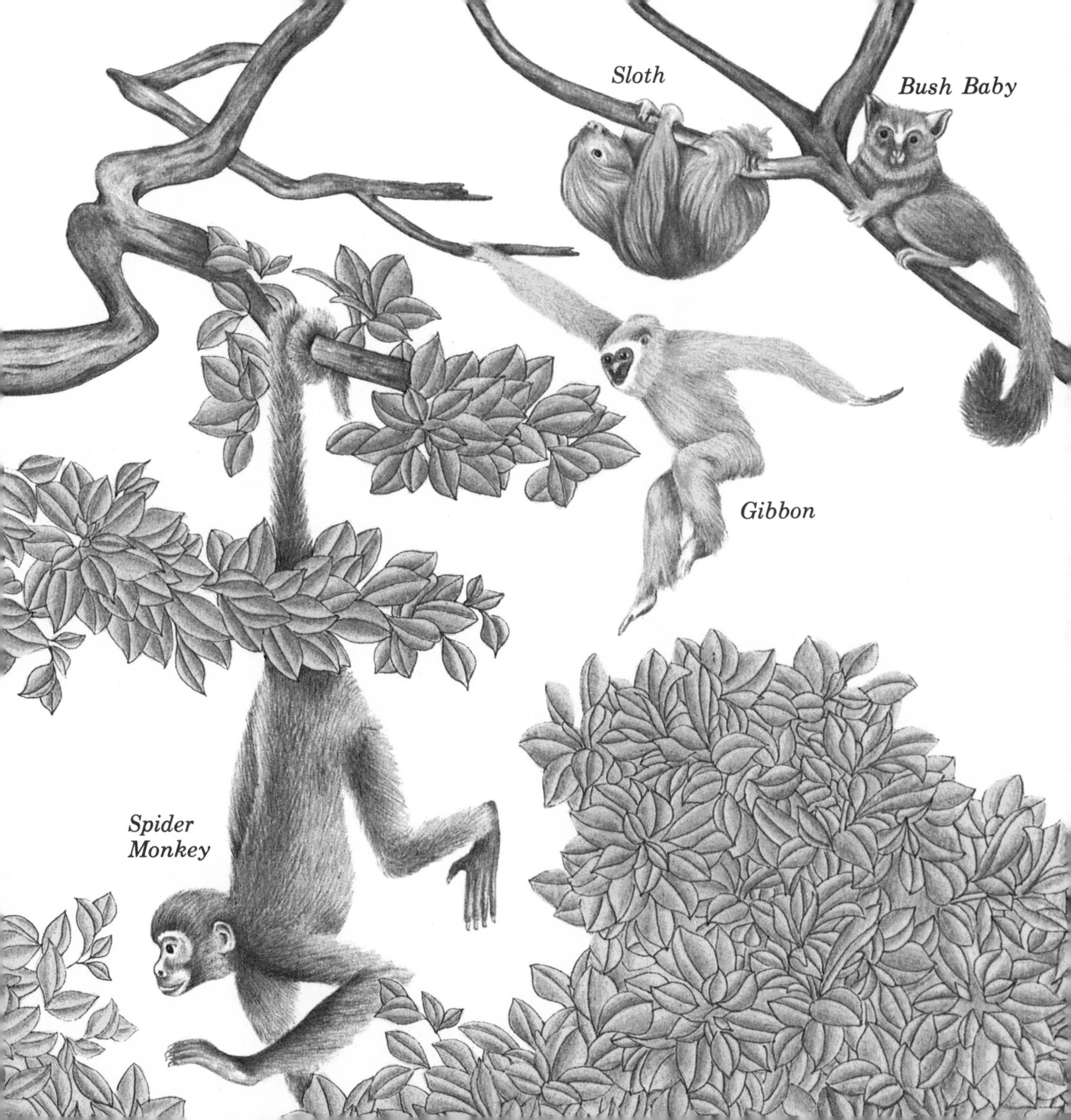
Sloth
Bush Baby
Gibbon
Spider
Monkey

But MAMMALS living in the sea
Porpoise
Sperm Whale
Walrus
Seal

have to surface frequently.

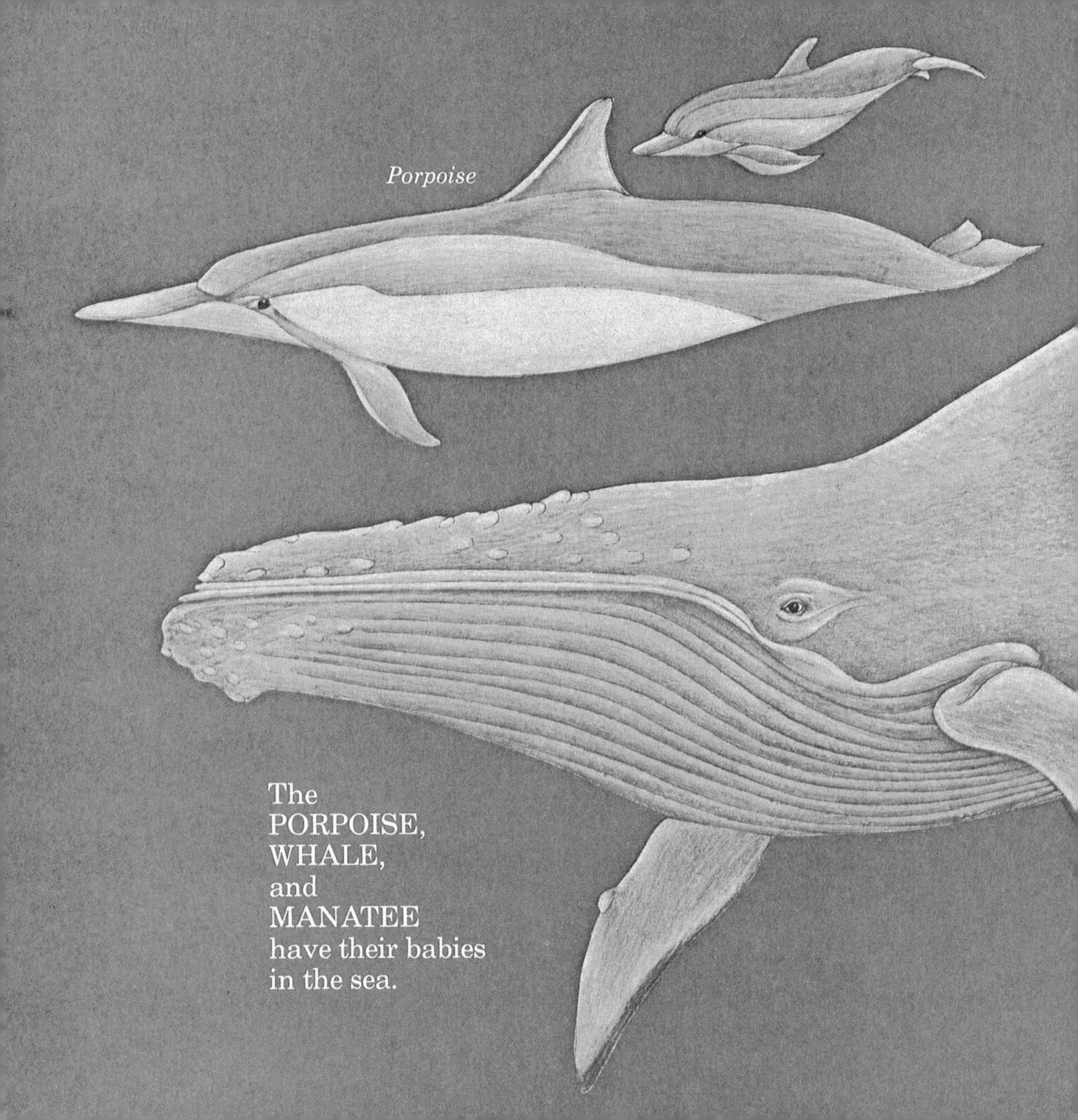

The
PORPOISE,
WHALE,
and
MANATEE
have their babies
in the sea.

Humpback Whale
Manatee

The WALRUS, SEAL, and OTTER prefer to leave the water.

Otter

Walrus

Seal
Walrus

These
are
prehistoric
but
they were
MAMMALS,
too.

Gomphotherium

Glyptodont

Their names
are very
long indeed
and
may be
very hard
to read.

The
largest
MAMMAL
is
the
BLUE WHALE.
The
smallest
is
the
SHREW.
Shrew

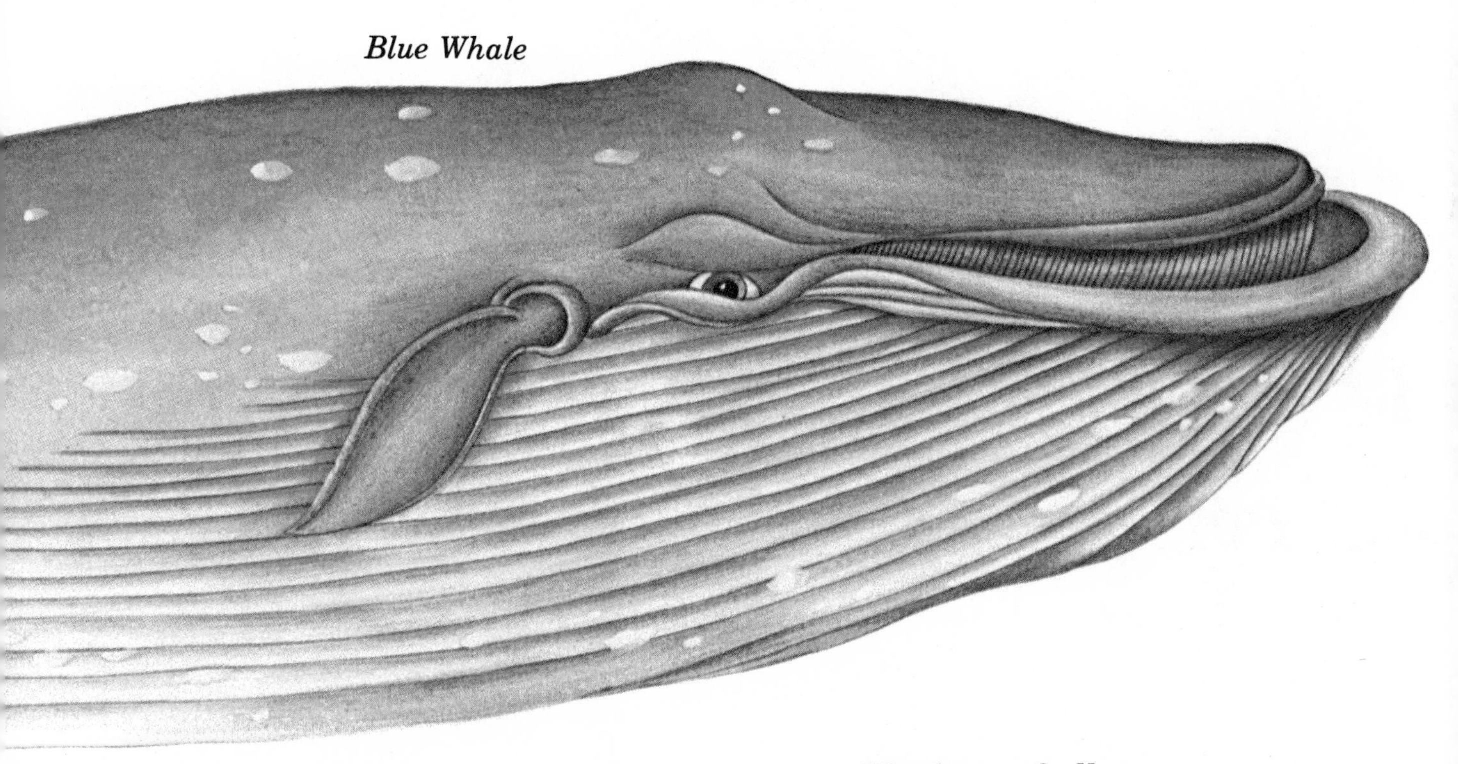

The best of all are...

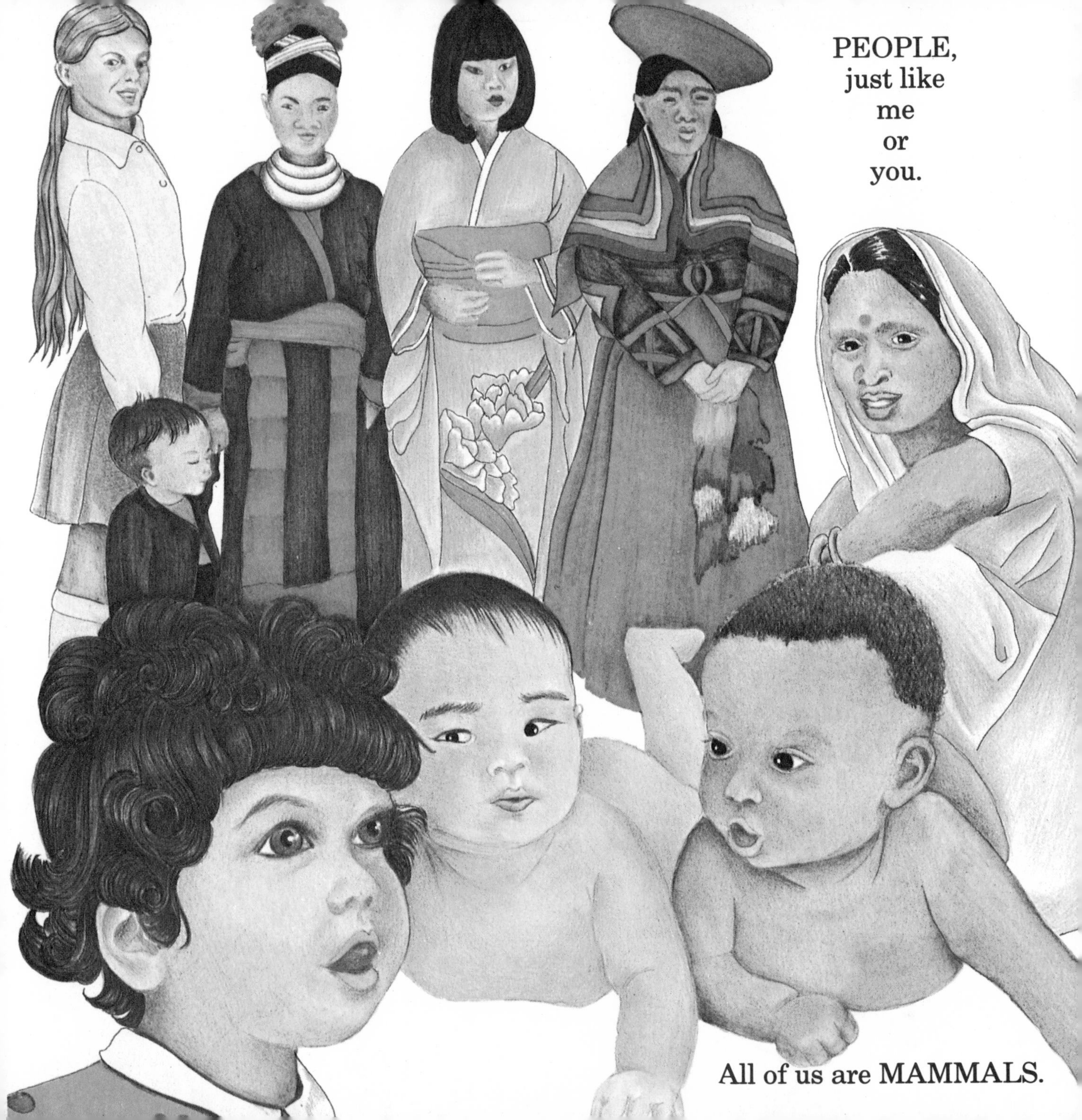

PEOPLE,
just like
me
or
you.

All of us are MAMMALS.

There's no more to discuss.
Everyone who's
born alive
is
VI · VIP · A · ROUS

Horse
Sheep
Pig

Winter, Spring, Summer, Fall...

Snowshoe Hare

a HARE'S hair changes with them all.